REALISING

THE GOD WITHIN

By G.C. Lebona

ISBN 978-0-620-88262-0 (Hardcover)

ISBN 978-1-990971-46-4 (Ebook)

ISBN 978-1-990971-47-1 (Paperback)

Photographs: GodsCreature ®

gclebona@majesticself.com

www.majesticself.com

YouTube: https://www.youtube.com/channel/UCQF6eRDOz6xdLyf9EGdl2Sg/videos

Cover and Interior crafted with love by the team at www.myebook.online

Written with all the love I can conjure

Dedicated to

ALL.

I AM.

"Live a JOYOUS LIFE. You are WORTH it."

TABLE OF CONTENTS

FOREWORD — 1

INTRODUCTION — 2

SHARING — 3

FOUNDATION: BIRTH AND RE-BIRTH — 5

BIRTH — 6

MOTHER EARTH — 7

METAMORPHOSIS — 9

EARTH BIRTH — 11

PLEA — 13

ONENESS — 15

FUNDAMENTALS — 16

TOOLS — 19

MEDITATION — 19

NATURE (APPRECIATION AND RECIPROCATION) — 21

EARTH — 22

RESEARCH — 23

SCHOOLS OF WISDOM 25

SCIENCE 25

ANCIENT WISDOM 26

RELIGION 28

REALM 32

HUMANITY 33

COSMOS 35

MATTER/DARK MATTER AND ENERGY 38

CHOICE 40

HUMAN CHALLENGE 42

ENERGY MIND/MATTER 44

FEAR 46

DETOXING / REPROGRAMMING 50

FRACTAL REALITY (HOLOGRAM) 52

CHALLENGE 54

THOUGHT ENERGY 56

MIND/HEART 58

PROGRAMMING 60

LOVE 62

DEPARTURE   66

WORD OF THANKS   67

ABOUT THE AUTHOR   **69**

FOREWORD

This book is written for ALL. with immense love.

It is for the strong willed. for the open minded.

It is for the ones who do not know madness.

The open.

Written with the love of the Universe.

The love of all my brothers and sisters.

The love of father and mother.

The love of the child in me.

The love of source.

The love of the infinite.

May it walk with you. Love always.

I am writing this to share with all humanity something that is bigger than words. Self.

The information is not for the purposes of teaching, but rather sharing and giving assistance to those who are willing to go further into all that I mention and interrogate themselves; or one who is already on their own path.

The information includes extracts from my personal path, which I am still on.

It is written with intention of sharing the key points, leaving you to choose your own personal path.

I share all this with ALL LOVE for humanity, for Earth, for myself.

Thank you for taking the time to read it. Thank you for being open minded. Thank you for your willingness.

May it reward you beyond measure.

What I am putting below to capture 'connection' to that which made us—Source / God / the Most High—is not a route map. It is not a routine to follow, but rather an understanding that is to be customized to suit you as a sovereign individual.

Note: I will be referring to That Which made Us as God from now onwards; do not fixate on the name. You can replace the word 'God' with the name you prefer or believe in.

- 'Himself' or 'herself' implies both himself and herself

- 'Reality' also means existence or life

- 'Connected' means 'aware' or in Oneness

- 'You' is interchangeable with We or Us, Yours with Ours

(The book is written both for the individual and for society as a whole—the path is very individual and the benefits are for the individual. However, the individual is a fractal of our society, hence their benefits are the benefits of society. This is the reason the topics are approached from a societal perspective at times.)

There are no rules and no direction to God, mainly because God is within you.

Hence, the 'path' to God is personal and customized.

What I am sharing is applicable to all, since we are all human. It requires for your own discernment and customization so that it becomes your way; your path.

Take what works for you and forge your own path.

The path, is our salvation. Our gift. Our majesty.

The challenge is that it is not something that can be taught or shown. It is something that is already there; something that is awaiting your acknowledgment. It is something you experience or live.

I am sharing this in Oneness and with all the love I can conjure. I call on all that I am, to guide me. To live within me. To be me.

This is a book about a human being and that which made it.

The book is hence about our reality and the being we are. Please take what you can and realize that you have to live it. You have to make it yours. Your way. I repeat this, as it is important.

Be yourself.

Much Love!

FOUNDATION

BIRTH AND REBIRTH

BIRTH

Everything that is alive, is born.

Everything that is born goes through some type of gestation or incubation period in a womb or egg. In the womb for humans and many other animals (mammals), and in the egg for birds, reptiles and many other animals.

The point is that, all come into being first in an enclosed or protected environment, where they are not 'aware' of who they are and the vastness of the world they have just entered.

All existence multiplies itself through this process of gestation and birth.

This process creates new life that is in the image of its creator (parent), but has its own traits and appearance although it carries the DNA, genes and essence from which it emanates.

During gestation, the new life has no idea or clue of what is outside of its womb or egg. All it knows is the inside environment and all it does or interacts with in this cocooned existence; living its life within the totality of the gestational sack.

Vegetation also goes through same incubation or gestation—called germination—in the Earth ground, from seed all the way to the plant.

This is a process of multiplying yourself for ALL that is alive.

Earth is called Mother Earth for the same reason. It is a gestation place where humans are growing incubated from the rest of reality (The All).

The story of creation says that God/s (superior being/s) came to Earth and created humans in His/their own image—in the image of God; by incubating their creation on Mother Earth, where it has been growing in incubation, believing that the incubated existence is the 'be and end all'. They now live with the belief that they were the only living beings in existence. As per all incubation, there is a predestined time where they will have to be born to go through a birth into the rest of reality or a new reality.

The intention of creating a new being is to enable for God to have a different experience of self. Human beings have been created with full intention of them 'birthing' into the bigger reality of existence some time in a predestined future time, as they develop and mature. This timeframe has exact points, just as it has for the incubation of a fetus in a womb. Hence, it is known exactly when the humans will birth.

This birth of humans is going to be a drastic change in their understanding of reality and themselves. It will necessitate a total change of the environment they are living in or an increase of what they have access to, their way of being.

This has been predicted by many ancient civilizations who foresaw these changes in their philosophies, religions, folklore, and history.

It has been predicted as a great time for humanity, but just like a birth of a child, a delicate and tremendous endeavor.

I am sharing everything in this book, to try to prepare you or give you a heads up; to make you aware and to 'equip' you with the wisdom or knowledge that will enable you to go through this transition period in peace, harmony, and excitement, instead of experiencing the changes as turmoil or fear.

We all need to prepare our hearts and minds by firstly releasing all that is detrimental to them, refilling them with LOVE, JOY, PEACE and HARMONY. We need to also acknowledge that we control our reality, which emanates from within us. We can make the transition less treacherous and a beautiful thing for all, where more spirits will opt to stay and experience the change alive, rather than mass exodus out of Earth (mass deaths) due to not being prepared to withstand the higher vibrations of Mother Earth as she gives birth to a higher dimension plane. A higher plane that is to be a planet for those who are born of spirit. We have to awaken to the fact that we are divine spirit beings and there's a process that we individually have to initiate and go through, to be born of spirit.

We have to acknowledge that we are part of a divine existence that is vast and eternal. If we are not prepared for that, the changes will seem like the end of the world to us. Our 'fearful' consciousness will fill our spiritual birth with fear, resulting in us creating fearful experiences as our reality (as co-creators).

Please be prepared.

Love yourself. Love everyone. Love everything.

Let love live within you. Realize that there is nothing but you. Be the God you are.

METAMORPHOSIS

Some life processes involve going through more than one birth process; birth from the womb or egg, living as one form of existence, and then being reborn (recreated) from this form to another form of life that is completely different, similar to the way a butterfly evolves from egg, for example *birth*-larva–pupa– *birth* -butterfly; same with frogs, ants, and more..

If you trace the history of humanity, it would seem that humanity also is a creature that is 'growing' through a process of metamorphosis; where in very long periods of time, our consciousness (being) is changing or developing. Our physical appearance, our 'way of being' and intelligence, changes in long periods of time, hence changing what we are.

If you look into what the ancient people say about the future and the reason they created everlasting 'calendars' of time that measure or track the cosmos. They understood that a human being grows through a process of metamorphosis. They marked future points at which humanity will 'change'—or be reborn.

The Mayans indicated with their calendar that life as we know it would end through the Equinox of 2012. They indicated that it will be an end of a cycle that will mean a major change in consciousness. It is a point where the Earth and consciousness of humanity will go through a major change—a rebirth (metamorphosis).

In Christianity, it is said that Jesus, an ascended master, said (John 3):

'Verily, verily, I say unto thee, except a man be

born of water and of the Spirit, he cannot enter

into the Kingdom of God.

That which is born of flesh is flesh, and that

which is born of the spirit is spirit.

Marvel not that I said unto thee, Ye must be

born again.'

This is pretty much straight forward; Jesus tells Nicodemus that a human being must go through the birth of water—a mother's womb birth. Then, one is required to go through another birth—one of spirit—in order to get into the Kingdom of God.

The masters are always trying to share with humanity the fact that you can go through a process of enlightenment (a spiritual birth), which will enable you to have access to 'more' of existence, access to the Kingdom of God, The All.

Surprisingly, humanity finds this difficult to believe, and do not really care much about this, considering that there is proof of the possibility of rebirth while alive on Earth, as shown by the butterfly and others. To me, this is proof that life can exist in one form, then change to a totally different form of existence, in the same lifetime.

For humans, it is a form of birthing the spirit you are.

EARTH BIRTH

The birth of Earth is more like an opening of a gigantic womb or egg that has been the gestation place for all of life within it (humans and other life forms).

The human being is to be born of spirit to enter the Kingdom of God, the realm of which humans on Earth are not generally aware of or have access to. The same as all that is growing in a womb or egg has no idea of the life outside of the womb or egg.

It is also said that the Kingdom of God is a realm with its own life—a way of being that is different; an existence by itself.

The larva knows only the area within the plant that it lives on, and believes this is all what life or creation is; crawling and eating leaves. It then undergoes a metamorphosis before it is born again as a butterfly. It now has a much wider understanding and access to existence. A butterfly is totally different from the larva; it eats nectar from flowers; it flies, and experiences more of existence.

The rebirth of a human being gives the human a much wider understanding and access to existence. It also changes what a human is, enabling other abilities or forms of being that gives one access to more reality—a reality that is totally unknown or inaccessible without this change (spiritual birth).

If you compare human existence with the metamorphosis of a butterfly, you can just imagine the vastness of 'change' and access to 'more' life that spiritual birth gives to a human being. This is what the masters are always trying to share with humans.

The calendar of the Mayans and the Christian Bible indicate that there will be a time in the future (from their timeline) where a human being will go through this metamorphosis or at the least will have the opportunity to initiate this process from within them.

It would seem that a human being has been given a choice to either go through this change while alive on Earth or not. However, there will be a period in the future where the Earth itself will go through this rebirth or metamorphosis. This will mean the Earth will now be a planet born of spirit and hence only humans born of spirit will be born and live in this planet.

All those who are only born of water and not of spirit will have to be born into a planet that accommodates for this level of beings. Earth would have ascended into a grid of beings that are born of spirit, joining the Kingdom of God. In some philosophies, it is said that the Earth will split into both realms. This is normally referred to in dimensions, as in moving from 3rd dimension to 5th, 6th, and higher. The higher dimensions are said to be realms for beings that are ascended; beings that have gone through the birth of spirit. Beings that know and live as spirits and have access to or experience of existence that is wider as compared to third dimension beings.

These are also referred to as realms that are of higher vibration; which means that the beings already born of spirit are vibrating at a higher vibration. Hence, they exist at higher vibration realms.

You have an opportunity to be born through spiritual birth while alive, as the masters did.

You are living in an era of the Earth where this is easier than ever before because Earth itself is going through spiritual rebirth or ascension. It is at a point in its timeline where it is changing to a higher dimension.

You have all the assistance that you will need in terms of all other beings that are already born of spirit being closer to you due to Earth being closer to their vibration. Like Jesus said, you can still receive assistance from him even when he is already only in a spiritual form (a higher dimension), his spirit is more accessible now than ever before (including other masters, Angels, Arch Angels; God Confluence).

The main prerequisite is that you must take the initiative. It is up to you. It is your life.

PLEA

I plead with you to love yourself; to love everyone, to love everything.

I plead with you to put all your differences aside.

I plead with you to work on yourself, to be a peaceful being internally.

I plead with you to release all anger, pain, and tension from within you.

This is not the time to be fighting anyone or anything. This is not the time for violence. The violence is a reflection of the turmoil within us.

This is not the time to be rioting for any reason. Do not be so easily offended to bring negativity out of you and putting you at low vibrations. Those are the exact opposite of the vibrations of Mother Earth.

The low vibrations (violence, riots, anger, fear) do not make you any different from what you are complaining about. All the help available will not be accessible to you, due to your low vibrations.

Let love live within you. Let your being be at peace. It is the only way you are going to live the peace you yearn for. It is the only way you are going to bring it into existence, as the creator you are. What you live, emanates from within you. Allow your inside to be peaceful and filled with love.

Your fears are terrified of the higher vibrations offered by the Earth; they are doing everything to keep your vibrations in a low state. They are doing all they can to derail your emancipation—your spiritual birth.

There is no place for fear in one born of spirit. Do not succumb; be still and listen to your spirit, no matter the provocation. Be LOVE. Allow for the love you are to be. Allow for the Oneness you already are.

ONENESS

There are basic fundamentals that I found important in order to give yourself a chance to have a better understanding of reality or 'connection' to God; to walk the path to Oneness.

It is important to firstly acknowledge that you do not know.

Discard everything you have been told or thought you believed about what you are, about God, and reality. All that you have been told or taught. It would be difficult to learn yourself anew, if you already 'know' yourself. The space provided by accepting that 'you do not know' is needed, to accommodate truth or new information. What you are in your quest to determine.

It is important for all you know or learn about being human to be always available to be 'changed', as you walk this path. You must not hold on to everything you 'learn' or hear with dear life. Your understanding will change, as you know more and more.

You have to be able to live with 'not knowing'. Live in peace with the fact that you do not know nor understand what you are, or reality.

You have to have the ability to change deep fundamental beliefs about reality. You should be willing to research all information yourself, and be willing to give all perspectives a chance. It is important to research all available informatin, even one you detest.

You have to LOVE yourself immensely, without reservations.

You have to know that there is NO reason good enough not to love yourself. None! No matter what you have done or been through, self-love has to be a norm. It is paramount.

You have to know that, That Which Made You (God), loves you beyond your understanding and without any reservations. He loves you because He made you; not because of anything you are doing, not doing, or need to do. Inherent love, because He lives through you.

You have to TRUST yourself.

You have to trust your DISCERNMENT of all information (knowledge or wisdom) you receive or conclude on. You have to trust your heart on discerning all information against it.

Minimize mainstream information, media or entertainment, as it tends to clog your mind.

You have to be thoroughly HONEST with yourself (easier said than done!), otherwise there is no point.

Do not be rudimental or 'scheduled' in your approach to realigning or relearning yourself. Do not make rules. Flow with what is in your heart.

Be patient with yourself.

NEVER, EVER JUDGE yourself.

Always know that the love you have for yourself surpasses everything. Always know that the love God has for you is unconditional. Do not beat yourself up for any reason; there is no reason good enough.

It is best not to put a timeline or an end game scenario.

There is no timeline but just for you to KNOW yourself. Always 'give yourself a break'. You are not in a race. You are just being open to that which you are.

Be willing to adopt and practice the wisdom that dawns on you, that resonates with you.

You must be willing to live with knowing that there is no end point.

It is a continuous growth cycle. However, the wisdom you adopt along the way is priceless. It is invaluable in creating or living a content life for you, your loved ones, and humanity.

You need to let go of labels we put on ourselves and on concepts, as they tend to come with other connotations. It is also important to let go of labels that promulgate separation e.g. race, culture, country, religion and so forth.

Do not take our uniqueness as what separates us.

You have to know that what you are looking for, is INSIDE you — not outside.

God is within you, not among what you are observing —the outside world.

It is important to learn how to go within yourself.

LOVE YOURSELF.
LOVE EVERYONE.
LOVE EVERYTHING.
BE OPEN MINDED.
HAVE AN OPEN HEART.
TRUST YOURSELF.

MEDITATION

It is a state of being rather than a process. Do not treat it as a DISCIPLINE with rules. There are guidelines; please use them. However, take these and customize to what flows with YOU.

Let it be relaxing; if it's not, then adapt your practice until it is. It should get your mind, body and emotions relaxed.

You should not be stressed about 'doing it right'.

It is easier when you are not afraid of quietness or nothingness.

It is easier when you already accept that you talk to yourself (small voice).

It is easier when you know that there is a place inside you.

It can be done anywhere, by anyone. It is not for sale. You do not need to be a GURU, and you can probably find one on your phone's YouTube if needed.

It is of great help, but not a necessity, to do it in natural environment (trees, flowers, birds, etc.)

It has no set time; even 5 minutes makes a difference.

Meditative music also assists.

Benefits:

It helps you slow down life. It gives the time to observe being alive.
It provides a window or door to your internal space, where God is (NB: Research and Individualize).
It allows you to CLEAR old programming that is detrimental to your well-being and prosperity and to reprogram yourself– this is critical.
It assists you to release all that is not serving your good—even old experiences fraught with pain, anger, grudges, jealousy and more.
It highlights the small voice inside you. This voice is important, as it narrates what you believe of your experiences, or what you think of yourself. It is the commentator of reality, managing your perception.
It makes you realize that you are not this 'small voice', and that you are able to view reality the way you want, negating the commentary of this voice. It also assists you in realizing that this voice is just regurgitating what you have fed (programmed) your mind through societal norms, culture, movies, school and other life-shaping experiences.
It enables you to reprogram this voice to be more in line with who you are, and to have a more balanced view of your experiences. It equips you with the bravery to be yourself, and not be lost to all society norms, beliefs, and limitations.
It gives the opportunity to teach your 'small voice' NOT to speak on behalf of third parties or society, and not to judge yourself.
It provides an opportunity for you to program your 'small voice' to be loving toward you, to have compassion for you or anyone else.

SUN

The power of the SUN and its effect on humanity is UNDERRATED.

Give yourself a chance to be in the sun at the least for some minutes daily, as per the allowance of your life and geography. ENJOY!

Benefits:

It energizes your body and gives you a chance to appreciate the gift that is the Sun. Thus, making you more aware of the beauty of your reality, and to escape the mundane.
The sun is the primary provider of energy your body utilizes. All plants need the sun to grow vegetables or fruits you eat, all animals that you eat get their energy from eating plants, fruits.
The sun's rays are part of the cosmos and carry all the changes that take place in the cosmos, bestowing your being with these changes. As the sun is the primary supplier of energy to your body, changes in the sun mean changes in the rays (energy) the sun emits, changes in energy provided.

NATURE (APPRECIATION AND RECIPROCATION)

Take walks in a garden, forest, or park.

Let it sink into you that nature is ALIVE, like you. You are sharing a realm with nature. It serves you; appreciate that and serve it.

It has a calming effect on your being. It gives an opportunity to experience yourself away from it all, where you have a better chance of enjoying clarity about who you are and how you want to experience life.
It makes you realize how majestic reality is, how magical it already is. It helps you awaken from taking things that have naturally been given to you for granted.
It enhances your understanding that you are truly loved by God to bestow so much on you. All for you.
It gives a chance for you to see how cooperative nature is.

EARTH

Realize that the Earth is a LIVING being or entity, just like you.

You are part and an aspect of the Earth, and it is part and an aspect of you.

(So within, so without)

Imagine all the cells and organs inside you carrying on with their existence as 'independent beings', just like humans on Earth. Now, imagine they did not know that they were part of the Oneness that is you. All the cells believing that they were independent and separate from each other and the whole, with no cooperation, but rather competing with each other.

Enjoy the LOVE of Mother Earth and reciprocate it.

It assists you to realize that you are not a victim of the planet, but rather loved very much by Earth, which sacrifices so much of itself to nurture you.
It makes you realize the patience in the love of Earth for humanity, like a mother to her children. Love them no matter what they turn out to be or do.
Realizing that the Earth is alive is a big step in assisting you to realize that all is alive and hence having a better understanding of reality and yourself.

RESEARCH

- Read up as much as possible.

- Carry the intent of knowing yourself without any preconditions; the knowledge will come to you.

- Never be afraid of information; you are bigger than it.

- Research as many vast and variable viewpoints as you can.

It makes your 'understanding' personal, broad and tested.
It enhances trust in yourself.
It solidifies trust in what you believe about reality and life

.

SCIENCE

Quantum nature of Reality

- Quantum mechanics

- Quantum Physics

- Quantum Biology

- Hologram Theory of Reality

You have to read up a lot of perspectives on this subject, including the bulleted headings. The key factor being that, the more scientists understand about quantum science, the more it reveals that our reality or universe is nothing like the Newtonian Science explains, meaning nothing like what is mainstream knowledge and understanding of reality as taught at schools and universities. Quantum science has also shown that there is no separation in the universe or cosmos, all is connected and hence One.

You will learn that at the smallest or core of everything (reality), there is NO matter. Not even our bodies, Earth, nor cosmos is matter. It is all energy.
We exist in energy. WE ARE ENERGY.
Matter is brought into being by consciousness. That which WE ARE.
We are the holders of the realm. We bring matter and material into being.
We are co-creators of our reality.
We create to experience the energy we are, just like God, as God lives within us and lives through us.
There is no separation; everything exists in one connected 'web'.

ANCIENT WISDOM

Firstly, acknowledge that ancient societies were more advanced in many respects than today's civilization. They have left enough physical evidence to prove this in the form of the pyramids, cosmos calendars, and Stonehenge, to name a few.

It is not debatable that ancient societies (Egyptians, Mayans, Indians) knew more about reality than we do now; or at the least understood reality differently compared to now. Please go and read their writings or books about them.

Read up on their understanding of what reality is, and what human beings are. Read up on their explanation of where human beings come from, and on fundamentals of their understanding of the cosmos and how it was formed. Read up on their history and recitation of their experiences that we would consider 'magical' or 'out of this world' if they took place today.

Benefits:

The idea is to realize that reality or history is not as linear as we are told to believe. It will also help you realize that 'magic' is merely something we do not understand, yet it is a norm for other civilizations.
You will also realize that we are not as 'advanced' as we believe; there has been more 'advanced' civilizations and beings on Earth before us.
The idea is to also get comfortable with the knowledge that there are other beings, as the ancients explain when talking about the origins of humans, and where they got their wisdom to be that 'advanced'.
Do not be afraid of the notion that there are other beings, they would have long taken Earth and obliterated us, if that was in the cards. They couldn't be waiting for us to get more advanced so that we can give them a good fight? Ridiculous! Leave fear out of your being.
Do not get swallowed up by all the history. It can become all-consuming, as it is so vast. The idea is to grasp that, there is more to life than what is generally accepted or known.

RELIGION

This can be an emotive subject for many people. I want to say upfront that I respect all human beings and their right to choose to believe anything they want.

I also want to ask all to please take responsibility for what you believe about reality. Do not let someone else define reality for you. It is your LIFE. It is not about your religion or groupings. It is an individual path or experience.

It has to resonate with you. This is why it is important for you to trust yourself, and your discernment of reality.

It is disenfranchising to say that you do not have the 'wisdom or know-how' to make up your mind on what you are discerning about reality or God. However, you believe that someone else CAN and MUST do it for you.

Do not give away your right and freedom over the most paramount of things away so easily: Your existence and life!!!

You have a right to discern everything about what you are told about who or what you are, about reality. It is your life. Trust yourself. Trust your heart.

Do not equate religion with God; they are not the exact same thing.

Realize that within you is all that you need to know about who you are and why you are here.

Benefits:

> You can acknowledge and accept that there is no one that is going to connect with God on your behalf; it is your responsibility; your right!

> You can acknowledge and accept that this is an individual matter, just like you 'arrived' into this realm alone. It is your LIFE to live. It is for you to experience and learn all you are, while alive in this realm.

> You can acknowledge and accept that no one knows you and what you came here for, more than yourself. IT IS ALL IN YOU.

> You can be empowered to take responsibility for your life, your existence.

MASTERS (Jesus, Buddha, St. Germain, Sanat Kumara, Lord Lanto, Mary, and El Morya.)

The masters incarnate to teach about reality and what a human being is, not to carry the responsibility for our lives.

They are always leaving behind the wisdom of their paths, in order for humanity to learn from them.

We tend to end up worshiping them and treating them as if they never took a human form to do what they did. Hence, we never see ourselves doing the same thing they did in realizing the God in us, initiating our spiritual birth.

Masters go through an 'awakening' process themselves, where they had to 'connect' or be 'aware' of God while in human form. They do this to be examples to humans and always share the information of how they 'connected' to God, what it means to be 'connected' to God, the wisdoms and virtues of being in Oneness, and all the benefits.

Realize that you are not 'connected' to God as the masters are, they cannot connect on your behalf. They connect and 'create' a path that you can follow, but it is still up to you, to follow or not—to 'do your part'.

Jesus came and created a path to the Kingdom of God for humans; a path that you can follow. He left you teachings of how to walk the path and get into the Kingdom of God. This was his purpose. It is not a matter of Jesus being 'connected' to God and now you are 'saved'. All you have to do is go to church and proclaim that you are 'Saved, in Jesus' Name', then go back and carry on with living your life, ignorant of the wisdoms of the path he left for you. That is a misunderstanding on your part.

Jesus did not come to Earth to die for you so that you can worship him. It was so that he could show you what you are; to show you your majestic self, and show you what is possible. He came to make it easier for you; to share how to reach the Kingdom of God. He even said that you would be capable of more than he has shown you—in this future we are living now.

In Matthew 14: 22 – 33, Jesus walks on water to go to his disciples whom were in a ship on the water. Peter asks Jesus if he can come to Jesus on the water. Jesus tells him to come. Peter then walks on the water to go to Jesus, until 'he saw the wind boisterous' and became afraid and started to sink, but Jesus saved him. The point here is that Peter did walk on the water too, to show you that the 'walking on water' is not exclusive to Jesus, but can be done by other humans. Peter started to sink due to fear and disbelief.

The masters leave a template or trail in the realm every time they incarnate and 'awaken' themselves in human form. This is so that we know what we are. Every time they do this, it leaves a 'trail' in the realm, which makes it easier for those who do the same thereafter, as there is already a 'template' or 'path' in existence. The first time is always the hardest.

The path is ALWAYS yours to walk. You have to do it for yourself. It is individual. It is customized. It is the reason for incarnation.

The masters come to show the 'way'. They have come and gone; you still do not automatically 'connect'. You must also do your part, for yourself. It is just easier if you have help. This is why Jesus says you will reach his Father through Him, through EMULATING him, and letting his spirit live in you. It is because the spirit you will be 'connected' to is the same for all the masters, the Spirit of God—Oneness.

Take responsibility for your path/connection, it is not a group/association thing. It is individual. It is the reason you have incarnated, to 'connect' to God while alive. To learn and fulfill all your lessons.

All the masters are always striving to share this with you.

Always know that you are not doing this alone. You are never alone. You have majestic help, God in you.

You need to get to a point where you realize and accept that reality is more energy than material. It is more of an advanced hologram with fractals. This is why 'so within, so, without'

Energy cannot be destroyed or eliminated, hence does not 'end'. It just transforms and changes form, from one form to another.

This is the reason why you do not just materialize (incarnate) in this realm from nothing. You are emanating from one form to a human form. The same applies when you die, you are transforming from a human form to another form of self (energy).

Consciousness is what is molding energy into the material forms we see, our bodies, the Earth, sun, moon, planets, and the cosmos as a whole.

The infinity of the cosmos is an indication of the infinity of the energy that The All or God is.

We are consciousness; hence, we are the molders of the reality we see as material. We are co-creators of the material world.

Our origin stories vary in terms of religion, and ancient wisdom, but at a higher level, they are more or less the same story.

The ancient scripts talk about a time when beings or gods came to Earth from out of space or dimension. It is believed that these beings created humans by modifying Earth based beings and animals using spirits from the gods (themselves). There is a story that takes this further in saying Earth is a garden whereby beings from different parts of the cosmos agreed to give their DNA or essence to be stored on Earth, to create a living library of the cosmos.

Religion (Christianity) says God created a human from Earth dust into which he placed the Spirit of God (Themselves), hence creating the human in their own image.

The stories imply periods in between, where the human being is twigged to make better and better over long periods of time. This is done mainly with the humans being unaware, with some people believing this to be still taking place now.

There is also a story that says that we are spiritual or Etheric beings that have been creating material existence over millions and millions of years, and we are now in a period where we are to remember our original self as spirit.

There is also a story that says human beings were created by advanced beings (gods) that came to Earth from another planet in order to mine gold. They created human beings to use as laborers to mine the gold for them. The story states that due to their internal politics and fights, the God that created humans gave them more than what the leader of the gods bargained for. He gave humans the same spirit that lives within the gods, and made it dormant to awaken at a later stage.

In all the stories, we are made of the spirit or energy of God. God is experiencing this realm through us.

God is within us. We are holders of the God energy and spirit. We are the consciousness. We are the molders of reality. We are co-creators.

God split Himself in order to be able to 'experience' Himself, hence that which is 'experienced' and the experiencer are the very same being: ONENESS.

We are the ONENESS.

God is The All. everything there is.

In the beginning there is ONE, then the Oneness split into two in order to 'experience' itself. Then splitting further into many, so that God can experience all potentials of being.

In the beginning there was ONE, then there was the BIG BANG. As it is said.

Then there was the cosmos, that which we 'see' (matter) and that which we do not 'see' (dark matter or energy). All ONENESS.

Earth and humanity are infants in this cosmos; most parts of the cosmos are far older than Earth. The consciousness that has been holding these parts into being is far older than human consciousness. Hence, any being (consciousness) from the older parts of the cosmos is far older than humans.

There has to have been consciousness (beings) to hold the cosmos into being, otherwise the cosmos would only have come into existence when human consciousness began. It means that the cosmos has only been in existence since the creation of humans. This is not true, as the cosmos has been found to be in existence for far longer than humans. The interesting thing is that energy cannot be created or destroyed; hence, the consciousness itself is not new, but rather its formation into human form is new.

The gods created humans by taking something from the Earth and infusing it with their own essence (Spirit of God/consciousness), hence creating humans that are in their image. The Spirit of God is what is living in the Gods and in humans. It is just split further to create humans. However, it is the exact same spirit. The gods have hence grown, or planted, the Spirit of God, further splitting God into a different form of being to provide for a different perspective of experiencing self.

Human beings are earthlings, grown on the grid of Mother Earth, under her hospice and nurturing.

The cosmos has many other planets with beings (consciousness) that are also different splits of God, as God is continuously 'growing' or splitting into many.

The parameters or laws of each planetary systems are different and unique to the specific system in order to give God a unique perspective of self as per each.

All beings of the cosmos are all but splits of the same God (consciousness or energy). ONENESS…

The entire cosmos is alive, and continues to grow. It is building and destroying all the time, just as a human body with cells growing and dying continuously.

Spiritualists believe the cosmos breathes in and out, meaning it is going out of itself and coming back into itself continuously. It splits with the exhale and then experiences Oneness with every inhale, hence continuously going in and out of itself.

It would seem as though human beings have grown enough to be in Oneness with God or the time for that has come. The time has come for humanity to join in Oneness with all other older beings, all as representations of God or Oneness; hence, the

increased opportunity or accessibility for humanity to
go through spiritual birth.

MATTER/DARK MATTER AND ENERGY

Matter is said to represent about 5% of all energy in the cosmos, with 95% being 'dark matter + dark energy'. Dark matter and energy are not visible to human beings. They are known to exist by scientists, but have never been really isolated, measured, and understood. It is just known that they exist by extrapolation from what is known, with experiments being done even now to try isolate and study them.

This means 95% of God (consciousness or energy) is not visible, nor understood by human beings.

This means 95% of what we are, we do not know nor understand. We have no cognition of 95% of what is.

We are MORE of what we do not see or recognize than what we do, by far.

We are that majestic and powerful, but we are not aware or awoken to this part of us. This is what the masters are trying to tell and show us about what we are. They always try to show us how to consciously be aware of the parts we are not accessing.

The thing is, we already are everything, the challenge is to be consciously in Oneness with this. We tend not to acknowledge our Oneness with The All (God). We do not function or work consciously with the 95% of which is part of you—part of consciousness.

The consciousness that holds energy into material being is in this 95% that we do not know nor understand. It holds the material 5% into being, consciously (deliberately) or unconsciously. In our case, mainly unconsciously.

Humanity is still sleep living. Not even aware of the possibility, even though many masters have tried to share this vastness.

There are probably innumerable beings (consciousness) in the cosmos who are aware or connected to Oneness; living in awareness, as they are old.

Is it not worth all your attention or energy to 'connect', to know yourself? To acknowledge your full control of your reality, to have deliberately control?

THIS IS WHAT THE MASTERS ARE ALWAYS TRYING TO TELL YOU.

Humanity has been given the gift of CHOICE—a choice to live your life as you will.

It is said that each planetary system is given its own unique laws or terms and conditions of being. Ancient texts, spiritual scriptures and life itself indicate that humans have a choice to live their lives as they choose. Human experience gives opportunity to return to the wholeness that we are or just live with the illusion of separateness. We have the choice to awaken to the gods we are or to rampage everything even to the extent of destroying ourselves. There is alternative history that states that we have destroyed ourselves before, more than once.

You are the molder of every aspect of your existence. You incarnate into human form, forgetting everything about all that I am attempting to remind you in this book, and much more. You are FREE to be and to do whatever you want, even destroy yourself unfortunately. But remember, energy cannot be destroyed; it only changes form.

You have a choice over ALL aspects of your existence. You do, however, need to put the effort to know yourself, what you are and how it functions. You need to put effort into connecting to the rest of you and be complete. It is the goal of life, the realization of who you are and your power over your life, the initiation of your spiritual birth.

It is the difference between creating 'Heaven on Earth' Or destroying ourselves and giving away ourselves to slavery.

IT IS THAT IMPORTANT

NOTE:

- All is fair in the cosmos. There is no good or bad.

- However, consciousness (God) is biased toward life, growth, love, joy, peace, harmony, and abundance—because that is what God experiences when we live out these virtues.

- You have all the support from consciousness or energy, if you are living or creating these virtues.

There is an urgent need to individually exercise our God-given right to choose. and choose life, love, joy, peace, harmony, and abundance for us individually, for Mother Earth and her creations, and for everyone; to enable a smooth 'spiritual birth'.

Love yourself. Love everyone. Love everything.

Let love live within your heart and mind so that our creations inherently contain joy.

- Our way of being is so contrary to LOVE.

- Our way of life is so contrary to LOVE.

- Our way of nurturing ourselves is so contrary to LOVE.

- We have turned parasitic to Mother Earth and everything given to us.

All this being a reflection of our ignorance—our unwillingness to learn and get to know ourselves.

The state of our world and our interaction with each other— with Earth and all nature—is a reflection of what is within us. It is a reflection of what we carry within us, what is imprinted; the hate, Pain, anger, lack, judgment, and separation, etc. We are the co-creators responsible for all our world and the reality we experience. We need to know and accept that, as it gives us the power to change the world. That power lies within us; not out there somewhere or with someone.

It is so easy to change your reality by changing what you hold in your heart and mind, by your belief of what you are and what you are capable of.

You can see yourself as a victim of existence, or you can acknowledge that you are the creator, and learn more about what you are and how you function. Use the knowledge to create the life you want.

Live your life with love, joy, harmony, peace and appreciation for life. Genuinely see life as a beautiful gift deserved to be lived joyously by all.

We all make up the grid of Mother Earth. We determine what life on Earth is like.

We do not have to organize or fight anyone. Just change yourself individually from within. It will change your reality; it will change our reality. It will change the world we all live in.

Christians talk about Heaven of Earth; you are the key to it. You always have been.

My plea with you is that you love yourself. love everyone. love everything.

Learn about what you are. Do not be told. Do not be despondent.

Forget about everything we see as different between us. Forget about everything that separates us. It is based on looking at 5% of what we are. We are 95% the same even from this perspective. In actuality, we are 100% the same being. We all are part of God, of Oneness.

The reality we want to live is within us. It is up to us to bring it into being. Through the emulation of LOVE.

KNOW YOURSELF.

The consciousness that is holding eternal energy into matter is within you, it is you (Spirit). What you hold in your imagination (thought/belief) and the emotion (heart/gut) you put to it are the machine of your creations.

Thought comes before Reality - always know, remember and respect this.

Emotions are a magnetic field around you, pulling what is in resonance with your emotions and repelling what is not – always know, remember and respect this.

This is why you have to Choose to be what you are, rather than to wait for the outside world to justify your knowing or feeling that you Are what you are/or want to be. Why give away such power, making living out what you know you are a decision of circumstance. You are giving away your state of being, the most important thing you own, to everyday happenings. Your sense of Self will always be a reflection of the world, not you.

You have to be, for your reality to be as such.

Your conscious, subconscious, super-conscious are immensely powerful and

precious. You MUST guard them with vigor. You must ensure that you are very selective of what you get through to them. What you get programmed into you. You maintain them, clear them of what you do not want and fill them with what you want in your reality.

What you keep in your heart and gut (emotion) is very important and powerful in determining what your life is. What your reality is. You must maintain this space, clear it of what you do not want and add what you want in your reality.

The state of your heart or being is very important and critical in determining your access to the rest of your 95%. What some people refer to as your 'higher self'. Love is the key.

You must release all negative energy we tend to keep within us—pain, anger, grudges, lack and more. No matter how important you may think it is to you, it is toxic to you and to your relationship with the God that is within you. Limiting You.

Fill your Heart/being with love, Peace, joy, abundance, Harmony; all your desires. Then be grateful for them; for being alive; for your life.

Have no room in your mind or heart for what you do not desire in your life—not even for the reason of 'planning' for it not to occur, or on what you would do if it occurs. Give no energy to things you do not want in your existence.

Believe that if things do not go according to your plan, you will know what to do. Do not plan for things not to go according to your vision.

All of this is fully in your control.

Fear is the worst enemy to being whole (GOD). The worst!

There is nothing to fear but fear itself. What a cliché, but how true!

You are what holds reality into being. You are the one introducing fear into your

Reality, all your fears are what you are manifesting—warped as it sounds.

We are a society that lives in an environment or have created an environment where we foster fear way too much. We introduce fear to ourselves even from as early as toddlers, maintained and reinforced till our death. We fear everything—even life itself to some extent.

We fear death, because we presume that's the end. It is not! You are energy. We fear death, because we believe that God does not love us enough and is going send our souls to some abyss or to hell. As if the God living within us is not love.

Our upbringings mentor us on how to be fearful. We create the things we constantly fear.

We create so much drama and distortion of reality, thus reinforcing our fears (proving them right). We forget that these distortions are there because we hold so much fear in our hearts and minds—not the other way around.

We fear lack, hence we create so much lack (poverty). We fear not being loved, because we do not love each other.

We are energy and our thoughts and beliefs build our reality. So, our belief or hold to fear is what is creating all the materialized things that justify being fearful to us.

We entertain ourselves with violence, fear, and all sorts of negative mindsets in our movies, sitcoms, adverts, news, books, music, and other types of media. We spill so much vile to each other on social media. This is all energy that has to come into being somewhere or somehow in our reality. We are co-creators.

Yet, somehow, we are surprised when our reality depicts all this fear with which we keep programming ourselves. What would cause all this negativity in our reality?

It is only because we do not know ourselves. We do not know what we are. We do not know how we function.

Do not teach your children to live in fear.

Take all opportunity and effort to release the fear that is programmed into you.

Do not entertain yourself with things you do not want to materialize in your existence. Your subconscious and operating system cannot tell the difference; it imprints them into your programming for real life; for your 'enjoyment', as you keep feeding it that.

Do not feed nor keep in your heart or gut all the things you do not want in your life, not even anger for or a grudge against someone else. The only person suffering from those emotions is you—not your enemy.

It is also important to remember that we are all one energy and share a reality, so we do affect each other. Hence, the better we treat each other, the better our reality will be.

You are that important.

Feed your heart and mind with what you want your existence to be; love, joy, abundance, peace, and harmony. Be what you want (your) reality to be.

Our collectiveness is the God that is creating our existence and world. We must take responsibility for it. It is not from some God sitting somewhere. We are also not a victim of the Earth or someone controlling us. We are allowing it.

We are the ones doing the creating; it is the way creation works. It is what we are. What is making us 'victims', is our ignorance to this.

I do not have to make you do anything; I just need to program what I want into your conscious/subconscious/superconscious, and you will bring it into being as you are what brings things into being – a Human Being.

You are the computer that has full control of its own programming. Take CONTROL of it.

Wake up!

We hold the key to our realm. We must collectively realize this. We are one. We must all love one another. We must want the best for all, for everyone and everything.

WE ARE THAT POWERFUL.

It is about loving yourself, loving those within your circle, and those you interact with in your life. All — including strangers, animals, plants –all existence.

It is about appreciating, and being thankful for all life.

It is not something you try. You either are or you are not.

Do not be despondent. Do not be fearful. Be patient with yourself. Be patient with all.

- You are not what you believe or think you are. You are MORE.

- You are not what you have been told or taught you are.

- Reality is not what you believe or think it is. It is You.

- Reality is not what you have been told or taught it is.

Find any method that works for you to release from within you—your heart / mind or being—all that is not representative of love.

Release all pain, bitterness, anger, trauma, jealousy, negativity, lack, and grudges.

Let it all go through you, but release it. Do NOT suppress anything.

Yes, it is easier said than done. You can use professional help to assist if you wish.

Release all defeating, disenfranchising, and victim-mode programming, thoughts, or beliefs. Release any voices that say you are vulnerable or have no control.

NB: Watch for implied programming in things you watch, listen, or follow. Be your own person—not a person who is told who or what they are.

LET LOVE LIVE WITHIN YOU.

LET ALL YOUR WANTS, DESIRES, and JOYS LIVE WITHIN YOU.

BELIEVE IN EVERYTHING THAT SERVES YOU.

LIVE THE LIFE YOU WANT FOR YOURSELF.

CONSIDER ALL DONE.

There are many techniques and ways to do the reprogramming. The most important is for you:

- to have room for new information about reality,

- to be relaxed and not take yourself so seriously, and

- to be playful like a child.

A child sees play as learning and discovery; see life this way. It makes it easier for you to reprogram the deeply embedded.

It is a process that challenges you deeply.

There is a viewpoint or understanding that says the Universe is a hologram made of fractals (the same pattern of wholeness is found at every scale) and holographic (the wholeness is present everywhere and within every entity), as well as synergetic (the whole is greater than and unpredictable from the sum of the parts).

This means that the smallest thing in reality has exactly the same pattern as the biggest thing in reality, and so are all the fractals in between. Also, the sum of the fractals is unpredictable and greater than the numeral sum.

'So within, so without.'

What is within that you call 'You - I am' is the exact fractal of what is without—The

All or God.

What you keep within your mind and heart will be reflected without (reality).

Even your body is a reflection (fractal) of the cosmos. The cosmos reacts or adapts to you and you react to the cosmos—as you have to remain the same fractal.

This is why the ancients studied the cosmos (Astronomy). It is because they had the wisdom of knowing that the changes in the cosmos are actually changes in consciousness, and therefore, changes in human consciousness. This is why there is a discipline called Astrology, which relies on the alignment of your being/birth with the state of the cosmos.

The ancients indicated that a pivotal point in the evolution of the cosmos would be 2012, when the old calendar ended; when humanity as we knew it ENDED.

When we reached a new age. The Age of Aquarius.

The Age of Revelations—revelation of yourself and your reality. This book is my part in doing that.

I will leave the rest to you.

The challenge is for humanity (You) to LOVE itself.

The challenge is for humanity to KNOW itself.

The challenge is for humanity to release fear.

The challenge is for humanity to release ALL INDOCTRINATION.

The challenge is for humanity to accept its majestic self. To believe.

The challenge is for humanity to accept that reality is energy. not matter.

The challenge is for humanity to accept that thought comes before materialization.

The challenge is for humanity to accept that we are CO-CREATORS.

The challenge is for humanity to accept that we are spirit having a human experience.

The challenge is for humanity to realize that the differences between us are consequential.

The challenge is for humanity to realize that the 'separation' between us is fictitious.

Our separation is the only way we can 'experience' ourselves.

It is the only way for The All (God) to experience more about self.

It is the only way we can 'enjoy' ourselves and enjoy the contrasts and unique forms.

We have all the keys. We are the keys. We are the co-creators.

We somehow have locked ourselves out of the Kingdom and thrown away the keys, so to speak. Some call this 'the fall'. There are different views on whether it was on purpose or by mistake.

Either way, it is time for us to wake up.

THOUGHT ENERGY

Our individual thoughts and beliefs about reality are the foundation of that which we experience as life. It is what crafts and fuels our reality and the perception we have about life. The collectiveness of our thoughts and beliefs is generally reflected in the world.

If you believe that you do not deserve nor have enough of anything, this belief will be reflected in your life. If we believe in lack of 'enough' food for everyone. then there won't be enough. This goes for any other resource.

Everything we believe through our programming WILL be our reality.

We do not believe things because they are that way. Things are that way because this is what we believe (co-create).

We are that POWERFUL.

The new age book and film, The Secret, tells you the same thing. This applies to everything that is our reality.

To change anything in our reality, we have to change what we BELIEVE about the very same belief, issue, or matter.

It is that easy to change our world, to create what we want, be it love, joy, peace, or even Heaven on Earth. It is the law

We currently believe in lack, violence, and many negative beliefs make up our society. We must individually and collectively change those to positive or empowering beliefs.

We believe in 'SEPARATENESS'. We must change that to truth. We are but one being or consciousness.

What you hold in your mind or heart is KEY, guard it with vigor. Let in only what you WANT to materialize in your life.

If there is anything you want to CHANGE in your reality or in your life, you have to FIRST change your thoughts and beliefs about it. This is PARAMOUNT.

You have to learn and teach yourself about how consciousness functions. PARAMOUNT

Our subconscious holds many programs about our BELIEFS, and what we create. Our subconscious is mainly on autopilot, it is taught everything it knows without a filter or discernment.

The subconscious is programmed from birth to death. Everything that it believes is learned, meaning it is vulnerable to negative belief about self being programmed into it. This is the norm with movies, TV, and more in the name of entertainment.

The subconscious is like a hard drive that holds core beliefs. Whoever molds those beliefs in society, molds society's reality, life experience, and creation.

Whoever programs your subconscious, molds your reality.

It is time that we understand HOW it is programmed, so that you take control of your OWN programming.

This is the only way to have SOVEREIGNTY over your existence on Earth.

Everyone has a God-given right to be in full control of their creation or life, for their creations to SERVE THEM (as long as there is no harm to anyone or anything else)

It is the only way you can eradicate what you do not want in your reality. It is the only way we can collectively create what benefits us all. If we do not exercise full control over our beliefs and thoughts. We are not in control of our life.

To show you how warped our belief or understanding of reality is, we believe that we can go to war to bring peace. THAT IS IMPOSSIBLE.

- Everything that interacts with our senses.
  (Watch, read, listen, hear, touch, smell)

- All concepts we accept as truth.
  (Science, religion, economics, history, cosmos, emotions)

- All group mentality.
  (Culture, customs, norms, laws, nationalism, civil, education)

The programming of society is the most important thing in our reality. It is what determines or has extreme weight on what we live.

You cannot change your life or reality without changing the programming or monitoring it. Restrain yourself from the type of programming you indulge or accept into your being. Make deliberate decision on what you are trying to program into you when engaging programs.

Anything else. Is a LOST cause.

Nothing exists in our reality that we have not CO-CREATED.

We are that POWERFUL.

The challenge is that we create a lot in our existence while ignorant to this—'ASLEEP'

We do not take responsibility for our reality, life, and existence. It is God. It's the authorities. It's the people in our lives. Anyone else but us. It is comforting, as we do not relate to what we have created.

The challenge is to accept that you bear responsibility for the world you live in. We all want to blame someone or something else because we all do not believe we would create such a flawed world. It must be someone else. If it were up to us, the world would be a better place; a heaven?

Well, it is up to us.

We also never want to believe that we are that powerful, because our self-worth is so low. We say God lives within us, but it's too much to say 'We are God'.

We always push away our divinity. It is too much.

We already ARE gods. Whether we accept it, or not.

We do not have to find it or fight anyone for it. It already is a reality. It is up to us individually to accept this to ourselves (or not), live IT (or not).

You can either use your godliness to create the life you want, or your godliness will be used to create a life that suits others and not you—but the creation still happens through you. Unplug from the controlled grid, with set norms and rules of creation. Be YOU!

We have even been told that we will awake to this wisdom and knowledge one day. We are now waking up to it.

Love is the answer. The key to heaven and God.
Love of self. Love of everyone. Love of everything.
Love without a subject. Internal inherent LOVE.

You have to hold love within your heart and mind. It is the 'connection' to the grid of ONENESS—the connection to God. This is why masters always tell humanity about love.

We have to all hold a vision of all of us (existence) being ONE—loving each other, loving all.

We have to all hold knowledge of the energy we are, being ABUNDANT and able to fulfill all of our needs and desires.

Remember, all is energy—infinite, unlimited energy.

We must all hold within us LOVE, JOY, ABUNDANCE, PEACE, FREEDOM. These are the virtues we want for ourselves and for humanity as a whole.

This is the way we are going to reprogram our reality (grid) to create the world we desire.

We must be WILLING to re-assess our beliefs about reality. This is the way we are going to bring 'Heaven on Earth'.

Please STOP believing that you have no power. Please STOP believing that you are not WORTHY of such power.

There is no one who is coming to 'bring' Heaven on Earth. The masters have come and gone. They have left us all wisdom and knowledge. It is up to us to ADOPT it and wake up to who we ARE, what we are.

We must individually take full responsibility of our beliefs about reality and our state of mind and heart. It must be only what we say we want our world and existence to be. No reason is good enough to hold what we do not want to create, especially not for entertainment. We can entertain ourselves with positive inputs/experiences/fun.

We must be willing to let go of fear, hate, and separation.

The individual holds and creates their own reality. The collective shares individual realities.

LET US NEVER MAKE THE MISTAKE OF BELIEVING THAT WE CAN VIOLENTLY TAKE PEACE. IT'S IMPOSSIBLE.

THERE IS NO NEED FOR VIOLENCE.

THE ENERGY YOU FUEL (HEART and MIND). COMES INTO BEING.

EACH ONE CAN CHANGE THEIR THOUGHTS, BELIEFS and HEART. INTERNALLY.

LIVE YOUR LIFE JOYFULLY

ASK. AND YOU SHALL RECEIVE.

YOU ALREADY HAVE.

BE aware OF THIS.

YOUR POWER.

KNOW YOURSELF

ALWAYS KNOW. GOD LOVES YOU

BEYOND YOUR COMPREHENSION.

ALWAYS KNOW. YOU ARE NEVER

ALONE. YOU HAVE NEVER BEEN.

THANK YOU FOR YOUR EFFORTS.

YOUR CONTRIBUTION.

IT IS APPRECIATED. BY GOD. THAT

WHICH IS YOU.

LIVING. ALIVE. THROUGH YOU.

WE ARE GRATEFUL.

THAT WHICH YOU PRAY / CALL TO, IS
WITHIN YOU.
KNOWS YOU.
LOVES YOU BEYOND MEASURE.
IS WAITING FOR YOU TO
ACKNOWLEDGE YOURSELF.
I LOVE YOU ETERNALLY AND MAY YOUR
LIGHT SHINE THROUGH.

MAY THE CONFLUENCE OF GOD,
AWAKEN FROM WITHIN YOU.
YOUR MULTIPLICITY.
YOUR ENTOURAGE.
GRANT YOU PEACE AND LOVE. JOY
ALL YOUR WHIMS AND WANTS.

All above information is provided with love and with hope that it sparks the love within you. It is written with intent to get you to want to know and experience more of yourself. It is written with clear intention to get you to research and practice what you have learned.

It is written to get as many human beings to work on themselves to enable for love to live within them; hence, ensuring that the reality we create is full of love, joy, and abundance for everyone.

It is written to alert humanity of the eminent time we are in, in our evolution, to give everyone a chance to work on themselves and take advantage of the gift of spiritual birth.

It is written to minimize or eliminate the unconscious creation of fear, tragedy and disease during this period of transition. It would be a wonderful time, if only humanity is going through it aware and deliberately.

It is written to free humanity from the control of fear.

If you have found the book to resonate with you and would like to know more or to interact with the author, please go to my website www.majesticself. com where you will find more information, my blog, my videos, forums, and the ability to arrange a time to talk to me.

I also will appreciate your feedback on the book. Please email gclebona@majesticself.com.

I am grateful.

WORD OF THANKS

I would like to take the opportunity to thank you for reading the book.

I hope it has piqued your interest and opened a new way of looking at who and what you are. I hope to have inspired you to be curious or interested enough to take this on, to do your own research, and walk the path for yourself.

My biggest hope is that I have been able to make you realize that you are love; that you love yourself immensely, and that you know that 'what made you' loves you inherently.

I hope you to consider how you treat yourself, how you treat others, and how you treat all nature.

I intend to help you realize that happiness is a choice and an internal work; it cannot be derived from anything outside of you.

I intend to help you realize and accept that you are not alone; you are never alone, and you have never been alone. I intend for you to realize that there is a lot that is in existence that is invisible to you, but is alive, loves you, and is part of you and you are part of it.

I intend for you to realize that you are living inside a reality that is alive, just like all your cells. The biggest realization being that it is all you.

May you have the zest to go further into what I have raised and make it your own. It is a treacherous journey, but one that is worth every step. It is what all souls who have been alive have dreamed of.

I want to also say that I do understand, if you do not resonate with any of what I have said in the book, I just hope to have piqued something in you, and that the information will one day be relevant to you as you hear it from a different perspective.

I love you and send you love, peace, joy, abundance and harmony. It is for you to accept them.

Love is the doorway to your divinity.

I am grateful.

ABOUT THE AUTHOR

I have always been a seeker of understanding of reality and human beings. I have always been open minded and not limited by society's view on reality, giving a chance to all other views on what our existence or reality entails. I have found that there is so much information outside of mainstream platforms about the story of a human being and the reality we live.

I studied the scientific developments that explain our reality—from quantum mechanics to the cosmos. I also read many journals and books on mathematical formulas explaining or detailing what mathematicians have found to be the pattern of our reality.

I grew up in a generally Christian family, but was given the room to go through the teachings with freedom to ask questions and find my own understanding. I also have the privilege of living in a secular country where I interact with people from different beliefs and religions.

I am an African and my culture gives the freedom to be able to accept that there are energies unseen that have a bearing on human existence. This helped me to be comfortable dealing with a subject that is soft and inherently requires acceptance of the unseen. I live in Africa, where there are still remnants of the origins of human beings at the Cradle of Humankind.

I have used all the knowledge and information I acquired through all the above avenues to write this book, which will be of assistance to the reader in opening up their mind to understand what a human being is, as well as our relationship to God and the reality in which we live.

I have written this book to give a perspective and not the detailing or directive. I have purposely left the detailing out in order to give you, the reader, the opportunity to research for yourself. Doing your own research will assist you in confirming my assertions or to build your own.

I have written this book because I believe the time has come for all humans to know themselves. I believe this will be the difference between having a blissful life with positive expectations of the future or having a life full of fear and an expectation of misery going forward. There is no longer room to just be in the middle.

The book is written to help you find perspective and balance, and to help you find the God within you to navigate these times. I have written the book with full belief and acceptance of the unseen.

The book is written for the love of humanity, for the love of life itself. The book is written because it is necessary.

GOD HUMAN

IT IS BUT LOVE THAT IS ETERNALLY
OMNIPRESENT.

JOY; PEACE; HARMONY

www.ingramcontent.com/pod-product-compliance
Lightning Source LLC
Chambersburg PA
CBHW022118050726

47591CB00002B/834